DISCERNMENT

LIVING
THE GOOD LIFE
TOGETHER

DISCERNMENT
acting wisely

study & reflection guide

Sue Anne Steffey Morrow

ABINGDON PRESS / Nashville

LIVING THE GOOD LIFE TOGETHER
DISCERNMENT: ACTING WISELY
Study & Reflection Guide

Copyright © 2007 by Abingdon Press

All rights reserved.

Scripture quotations in this publication, unless otherwise indicated, are from the New Revised Standard Version of the Bible, copyrighted © 1989 by the Division of Christian Education of the National Council of the Churches of Christ in the United States of America, and are used by permission.

This book is printed on acid-free, elemental chlorine-free paper.

ISBN 978-0-687-64344-8

07 08 09 10 11 12 13 14 15 16—10 9 8 7 6 5 4 3 2 1
MANUFACTURED IN THE UNITED STATES OF AMERICA

Contents

—1—

An Introduction to This Study Series

PSALM FOR PRAYING

Psalm 1:1-3

Happy are those
    who do not follow the advice of the wicked,
or take the path that sinners tread,
    or sit in the seat of scoffers;
but their delight is in the law of the LORD,
    and on his law they meditate day and night.
They are like trees
    planted by streams of water,
which yield their fruit in its season,
    and their leaves do not wither.
In all that they do, they prosper.

CHRISTIAN CHARACTER IN COMMUNITY

THE GREAT EARLY Christian theologian Augustine opens his Confessions with these famous words: "Restless is our heart until it comes to rest in thee." Augustine, who had himself led a life of distorted and disordered desires that left him frustrated and without satisfaction, eventually discovered that we only find satisfaction when we rest in God. We are created for life with God, and only through God's love will we discover the rest, wholeness, and fullness we most truly desire.

So how can we discover this fullness of life that we yearn for, especially when we try and try but can't seem to get any satisfaction? Ironically, we will only discover it when we quit trying so hard. Instead, we need to learn to rest in God, the God who loves us and embraces us before we can do anything. God's grace invites us to discover that we cannot earn love; we can only discover it in the gift of being loved.

So far, so good. But it seems easier said than done. After all, to receive the gift of being loved calls for us to love in return. And yet we lack the skills—and often the desire—to love in the way God loves us. As a result, as wonderful as it sounds to "rest in God," to discover "the gift of being loved by God," we fear that we are not up to the relationship.

In order to truly receive love, we want to become like the lover. So for us to truly receive God's love, we are called to become like God—and that sounds both inviting and scary. Become like God? This becomes even more daunting when we discover that this gracious, loving God is also the one who is called "holy" and calls us through God's love to be holy as well. Jesus even enjoins us to be "perfect" as our "heavenly Father is perfect" (Matthew 5:48). The task begins to seem overwhelming. How does this relate to the idea of resting in God's grace?

The wonder and joy of Christian life is that we are invited by God into a way of life, a life of abundance in which we learn to cultivate habits of desiring, thinking, feeling, and living that continually open us to the grace of God's holiness. The invitation to Christian life is an invitation to discover that "the good life" is lived in the light of God's grace. When we embark on a truly Christian life, we learn to become holy not by trying really hard but by continually being drawn into the disciplined habits of living as friends of God in the community of others.

This may seem odd at first, but think about it in terms of learning to play the piano. We're drawn by the desire to play beautiful music. But before we can play beautiful music, we have to learn basic habits: the position of our hands, the scales of the piano, the role of the foot pedals, and the rhythms of music. Over time, as we learn these basic skills, our teachers invite us to take on more challenging tasks. Eventually, we find ourselves playing with both hands, learning to master more complicated arrangements of music, and perhaps even integrating the foot pedals into our playing. If we practice the piano long enough, we will reach a point where it seems effortless to play—and even to improvise new music—in the company of others.

It's around this metaphor of practice that Living the Good Life Together: A Study of Christian Character in Community has been developed. Rather than to practice being piano players, this series of small-group studies is aimed at helping persons practice being Christian. Each unit of study is designed to move persons from understanding various aspects of Christian character to developing practices that reflect those aspects of Christian character to, ultimately, embodying Christian character in community. In other words, the idea is to educate the desires of heart and mind in order to develop, over time, patterns of living like Christ.

A billboard or bumper sticker would say it more succinctly: "The Good Life: Get It. Try It. Live It—Together."

Living the Good Life Together gets at the heart of the life God intends for us, particularly as it relates to others in community. Attentiveness, forgiveness, discernment, intimacy, integrity, hospi-

9

tality—these are some of the aspects of the life God intends for us. And they are the subjects of this study series.

STUDY FORMAT

The overall process of this study series is based on some of Jesus' own words to his followers: "Come and see" (John 1:39) and "Go and do likewise" (Luke 10:37). In each study, the first six sessions are the backbone of the "Come and See" portion. These sessions inspire and teach the group about a particular character trait of the Christian life. The second six sessions are the "Go and Do" portion. For these sessions, the study offers tools to help group members plan how to put into practice what they have learned.

"Come and See"

Session 1: An Introduction to This Study Series

This session is an orientation to the twelve-week study. It provides information about the Living the Good Life Together series and an introduction to the trait of Christian character addressed in that particular study.

Sessions 2–5: Topics in Christian Character

These sessions offer information about aspects of the particular trait of Christian character. The sessions will help group members explore the trait and will foster intimacy with Scripture, with others, and with God.

Session 6: Planning the Next Steps Together

In this session, group members plan what they will do together in Sessions 7–12 to practice the Christian character trait they have learned about in the previous sessions.

"Go and Do"

Sessions 7–12: From Study to Practice

In these sessions, group members will carry out their plans from Session 6, putting their learnings into practice.

USING THE RESOURCE COMPONENTS

The resource components of Living the Good Life Together— the study & reflection guide, leader guide, and DVD—and the group sessions function together to foster intimacy with Scripture, with others, and with God. This takes place through a broad range of approaches: reading, writing, discussion, viewing video, prayer, worship, and practical application.

Study & Reflection Guide

This book serves as a guide for individual preparation from week to week, as a personal journal for responding to all elements of the study, and as a planning tool for the "Go and Do" portion of the study. Becoming familiar with the following content sections will enhance the effectiveness of this guide.

Psalm for Praying

A psalm text appears on the first page of each session of the study & reflection guide. It is there for you to use as a prayer of invocation as you begin your study each day.

Daily Readings

Reading these passages each day is central to your preparation for the group meeting. Consider reading from different translations of the Bible to hear familiar texts in a fresh way. Ask what the Scriptures mean in light of the session's theme and how they apply to your own life. Be alert to insights and questions you would like to remember for the group meeting, and jot those down in the boxes provided in this study & reflection guide.

Reflections

The space at the bottom of each page in each content session of the study & reflection guide is provided for making notes or recording any thoughts or questions the reading brings to mind.

Lectio Divina

Each session of this study will include a prayer exercise called *lectio divina*, sometimes called "praying the Scriptures." The practice of lectio divina, which is Latin for "sacred reading," continues to gain popularity as people discover anew this ancient and meaningful approach to prayer.

In the practice of lectio divina outlined as follows, we listen, as the Benedictines instruct, "with the ear of the heart" for a word, phrase, sound, or image that holds a special meaning for us. This could be a word of comfort, instruction, challenge, or assurance. It could be an image suggested by a word, and the image could take us to a place of deep reverence or personal introspection.

It is important to note that like the biblical exercises in this book, lectio divina is about what is evoked in you as you experience the text. Now is not the time for historical-critical musings or scholarly interpretations of the text. It is time for falling in love with the Word and experiencing the goodness of God.

Step One: *Silencio.* After everyone has turned to the Scripture, be still. Silently turn all your thoughts and desires over to God. Let go of concerns, worries, or agendas. Just *be* for a few minutes.

Step Two: *Lectio.* Read the passage of Scripture slowly and carefully, either aloud or silently. Reread it. Be alert to any word, phrase, or image that invites you, that puzzles you, that intrigues you. Wait for this word, phrase, or image to come to you; try not to rush it.

Step Three: *Meditatio.* Take the word, phrase, or image from your Scripture passage that comes to you and ruminate over it. Repeat it to yourself. Allow this word, phrase, or image to engage your thoughts, your desires, your memories. You may share your word, phrase, or image with others in the group, but don't feel pressured to speak.

Step Four: *Oratio.* Pray that God transform you through the word, phrase, or image from Scripture. Consider how this word, phrase, or image connects with your life and how God is made known to you in it. This prayer may be either silent or spoken.

Step Five: *Contemplatio.* Rest silently in the presence of God. Move beyond words, phrases, or images. Again, just *be* for a few minutes. Close this time of lectio divina with "Amen."

(Adapted by permission from *50 Ways to Pray: Practices From Many Traditions and Times*, by Teresa A. Blythe, Abingdon Press, 2006; pages 45–47)

Faithful Friends

True friends in faith are those who can help us hear the voice of God in our lives more clearly. They act as our mentors, our guides. At times they weep with us, and at other times they laugh with us. At all times they keep watch over us in love and receive our watch-care in return. Having a faithful friend (or friends) and being a faithful friend are at the heart of what it means to live as a Christian in community for at least three reasons:

- Faithful friends can at times challenge the sins we have come to love.
- Faithful friends will affirm the gifts we are afraid to claim.
- Faithful friends help us dream the dreams we otherwise wouldn't have imagined.

During this study, each group member will be invited to join with one or two others to practice being a faithful friend over the course of the twelve weeks and hopefully beyond. While there are no "mystical" qualifications for being a faithful friend, what *is* required is the willingness to be open to possibilities of guiding another person or persons into a deeper and richer experience of Christian living. Like all aspects of the Christian life, this activity of being a faithful friend is a discipline, a practice.

A key decision faithful friends will make is how to stay in touch week after week. Some may choose to meet over lunch or coffee or take a walk. Others may choose to use e-mail or the telephone. Whatever the means, consider using the following questions to stimulate an ongoing conversation over the course of the study:

- How has it gone for you, trying to live the week's practice?
- What's been hard about it?
- What's been easy or comfortable?
- What challenges have there been? What rewards?
- What kinds of things happened this week—at work, at home, in your prayer life—that you want to talk about? Has anything affected your spiritual life and walk?

There's an old African proverb that says, "If you want to go fast, go alone. If you want to go far, go together." In the end, a faithful friend is someone who is willing to go the distance with you, following Christ all the way. The aim of this feature of the study is to move you further down the way of Christian discipleship in the company of another.

DISCERNMENT: ACTING WISELY

Discernment is the Christian character trait featured in this study of living the Good Life Together. Sometimes we define *discernment* as seeking God with all our senses—taste, sight, sound, smell, and touch. It means using all our senses to discern the presence of God—and to do this with clarity. Such discernment informs wise actions in our daily lives.

Our study of discernment will be far ranging. Discernment is critical when it comes to something as daunting as putting a country back together after years of great violence. Desmond Tutu, writing of South Africa's struggle to recover from apartheid, refers time and again to the hard work of discernment. But putting a single life back together after tragedy has taken its toll also demands great compassion and careful discernment. Wisdom gained through discernment is critical in both situations.

Discernment is about big things, about life-changing events and decisions. But discernment is also about everyday things. In which direction do you set your feet in the morning? How open is your heart to the gift of birds and trees and song? How does the pace of life you keep each week allow small acts of compassion and kindness?

In great things, in small things, God calls us to discern God's presence. Sometimes discernment comes quickly, with inspiration and sure knowing. Other times, it comes slowly, painstakingly, and even seemingly not at all.

The Bible is the story of God's people's attempts to be faithful by discerning God's presence in their faith community and in their individual lives. Sometimes these stories are full of irony and almost comical. Sometimes they are dead earnest, filled with tears and struggle. But always, God's promise to be with us—in clarity and in confusion—is true. We are not left to ourselves alone. The challenge of the faith is to discern, to understand just where God is, even when we don't feel God's presence; and then to act with faith in God's presence.

This study is an opportunity to learn about discernment in the Scriptures and to discover how to seek and discern God's presence in our lives, our work, and our world. It is about learning how to discern so that we may learn how to join God in the work and world where God is. "Discerning God's Presence in Our Midst" invites us to take a close look at our daily lives and find God close around us. "Discerning God's Presence in Our Work" explores work as something done—with discernment—for the common good. "Discerning God's Presence in the Shadows" examines what it means as a person of faith to experience the absence of God, and to be able to adjust our seeing so that we may be ready to recognize God's presence. "Discerning God's Presence in Our Habit of Being" encourages us to carry the practice of discernment so closely that we carry our awareness of God with us wherever we are and that we act out of that awareness. "Planning the Next Steps Together" facilitates a group planning process for putting into practice what the group has learned about discernment. All the sessions help us to deepen our relationship with God and to practice discernment as a spiritual discipline.

—2—

Discerning God's Presence in Our Midst

PSALM FOR PRAYING

Psalm 8:1, 3-6, 9

O LORD, our Sovereign,
> how majestic is your name in all the earth!
You have set your glory above the heavens.
> . . .
When I look at your heavens, the work of your fingers,
> the moon and the stars that you have established;
what are human beings that you are mindful of them,
> mortals that you care for them?
Yet you have made them a little lower than God,
> and crowned them with glory and honor.
You have given them dominion over the works of your
> hands;
> you have put all things under their feet.
> . . .
O LORD, our Sovereign,
> how majestic is your name in all the earth!

DAILY READINGS

DAY ONE
Isaiah 11:1-3 *(A spirit of wisdom and understanding)*

DAY TWO
Romans 12:1-2 *(That you may discern what is the intention of God)*

DAY THREE
Luke 11:9-10 *(Ask, search, knock)*

DAY FOUR

Psalm 34:1-8 *(O taste and see that the Lord is good)*

DAY FIVE

1 Kings 4:29-30 *(God gave Solomon great wisdom)*

DAY SIX

Read the chapter on pages 20–24. You may take notes in the space provided at the bottom of each page.

Tuesday Morning, Commencement at Princeton

I walked over to the campus early as the half moon still shown about the top of the blossoming tulip trees, and the sun was just beginning to edge itself upward dispersing the dark. It seemed to me that the whole world was filled with the fragrance of mock orange and honeysuckle; and the town, though still asleep, held a sense of expectation for the day.

As I came through Blair Arch and across the space undergraduates call Alexander Beach, I heard the sound of voices singing, resonant, and I moved toward the song. It was the singing of workers, who were setting up folding chairs in front of Nassau Hall and raking the gravel and sweeping the podium and hanging the banners and checking the sound system.

God the Creator was moving through the space as certainly as the first rays of the sun danced through leaves of the elm and the oak, the presence of God who creates moon shadows and sunlight and humans for work and for song.

> O taste and see that the Lord is good!
> How do we come to discern the presence of God?
> And what is the nature of the God we come to discern
> and taste and see?

Glide Memorial Church in San Francisco

Glide Memorial United Methodist Church in San Francisco was on the brink of extinction in 1963. Glide was an outpost of ortho-

reflections

doxy with about thirty-five people in church on Sundays. That was the year the Reverend Cecil Williams joined the church as pastor and vowed to turn the tide.

"We had to take risk after risk to become an integral part of the community," Williams says. "The first step was to find members wherever I could find them. Outside the church were drug addicts and prostitutes, and I invited them right in. My wife, Jan Mirikitami, now San Francisco's poet laureate but back then totally unknown, began to read her poems in the Sunday service. We were off and running."

Today, Glide runs over fifty community service programs on a budget of $10.5 million. Religious services during the week draw homeless people who worship beside high-flying wheeler-dealers. Gays and lesbians are a visible presence at Glide. Glide was the first open and affirming United Methodist congregation. The gospel choir is a mix of people, all made in the image of God: blacks and Latinos, whites and Asians.

"Why not?" asks Williams. "I'm a mix myself!"

God the Redeemer moves through Glide as the soup is served in the evening to all who come and as the HIV/AIDS support groups meet on Thursdays at noon and as the people gather to pray and to sing and to hear the Word, to worship God together.

O taste and see that the Lord is good!
How do we come to discern the presence of God?
And what is the nature of the God we come to discern
and taste and see?

reflections

ANNA, OUR DAUGHTER'S FRIEND

Our daughter Ruth has a friend, Anna, who during her fresh-men year in high school had a stroke while riding her bike home from field hockey practice. Anna, found on the side of the road by another biker, was rushed to a local hospital and eventually trans-ferred to Children's Hospital of Philadelphia (CHOP).

Anna's father said to me later, "Astonishing how one minute I am putting away lawn furniture in the basement for winter storage and the next minute we are following a police car and an ambu-lance—terrified for our daughter's life. Now our hope is for full recovery, though she is not able to move her right side easily. It seems like the whole town knows and cares and is praying for us."

Anna's field hockey team arrived at CHOP one afternoon to give her a cheer and updates on the last number of games. Anna's singing group came to CHOP to sing for her and all the other patients on her floor. Her progress was slow but steady. Her eye-sight and the numbness in her hand were a worry. Therapy began. It took concentration and courage.

"One night when we came back from the hospital," her father told me, "we were so tired and hungry that we didn't have the strength to stop for groceries or sit down in a restaurant. We knew we didn't have much to eat at home but went there anyway. When we arrived, there was this gorgeous big lasagna waiting for us, with aromas of tomatoes and basil, all brown and crunchy on the top. It was from someone we didn't even know. Imagine."

God the Sustainer moves through the heart and hands and love of a near stranger with lasagna, and through the doctors and the nurses and therapists and chaplains of CHOP, and through friends singing and cheering and hoping and praying.

O taste and see that the Lord is good!
How do we come to discern the presence of God?
And what is the nature of the God we come to discern
and taste and see?

DISCERNING THE PRESENCE OF GOD

William James writes in his hallmark treatise *The Varieties of Religious Experience,* "Religion is the belief that there is an unseen order in the universe and our supreme good lies in harmoniously adjusting ourselves thereto."[1] Although the language is slightly antiquated, reflecting James's nineteenth-century New England education, the meaning is clear: Part of what it means to be human, to be religious, to be Christian is to discern the supreme good that lies in the unseen order and to respond by finding ourselves in the circle of that goodness. Paul puts it another way in Romans 12:2: "Do not be conformed to this world, but be transformed by the renewing of your minds, so that you may discern what is the will of God—what is good and acceptable and perfect."

How do we discern the presence of God? What is the nature of this God we discern? How do we explore further to discern God in our work and in our play, in the shadows and in the dark? Finally, how can we open ourselves to discern God in our habits of being, "to harmoniously adjust ourselves," as William James so aptly put it?

The Random House Dictionary defines *discern* as "to perceive by sight or some other sense, or by intellect." I hope we might use all of our senses to discern God—our sight, touch, hearing, taste, and smell. I got a sense of this discernment recently when a colleague related the following story:

reflections

23

When I was traveling through South Africa, the two senses that I use the least—my sense of hearing and my sense of smell—were brought to the forefront. We were riding in a bus on our way to do the day's work, when I heard the sound of children singing. It was a children's school choir, rehearsing outside. The children were in starched white uniforms and were singing toward the hills, and the echo came back like a bubbling brook of sound and harmony.

Later, as we walked from one appointment to another, I noticed a magnificent smell and looked up to see a blossoming bush. Other walkers stopped to admire the blossom, its sight and its fragrance. We smiled and greeted one another, then went on, our day enriched.

Marilynne Robinson teaches in the writing program at the University of Iowa. She wrote an award-winning novel, *Gilead*, which, if it is about anything, is about discerning the presence of God through the pleasure and pain of ordinary prairie life. She also has an exquisite essay on Psalm 8, in which she writes: "So I have spent my life watching ... to see, great mystery, ... what is plainly before my eyes. I think the concept of transcendence is based on a misreading of creation. With all respect to heaven, the scene of the miracle is here, among us."[2]

I hope that we, like Robinson, may discern plainly the miracle of God's presence among us.

PRAYER

Awaken our senses, O holy God, to your presence,
Awaken our sight, hearing, touch, taste, smell,
Open our hearts.
And we will sing your praises. Amen.

reflections

FAITHFUL FRIENDS: WATCHING OVER ONE ANOTHER IN LOVE

Use this space to record thoughts, reflections, insights, prayer concerns, or other matters that arise from your weekly conversations with faithful friends.

—3—

Discerning God's Presence in Our Work

PSALM FOR PRAYING

Psalm 86:10-12

For you are great and do wondrous things;
    you alone are God.
Teach me your way, O LORD,
    that I may walk in your truth;
        give me an undivided heart to revere your name.
I give thanks to you, O Lord my God, with
        my whole heart,
        and I will glorify your name forever.

DAILY READINGS

DAY ONE
Proverbs 31:10-31 *(The capable woman)*

DAY TWO
Micah 6:6-8 *(What does the Lord require?)*

DAY THREE
Romans 12:9-18 *(Let love be genuine)*

DAY FOUR

Colossians 3:12-15 *(Clothe yourselves with compassion)*

DAY FIVE

Luke 13:20-21 *(The kingdom of God is like yeast that a woman took)*

DAY SIX

Read the chapter on pages 30–34. You may take notes in the space provided at the bottom of each page.

CAMPHILL VILLAGE

I get up at six in the morning. I brush my teeth. I shave, wash, and get dressed. I walk over to the hall. I unlock the hall. I check my watch. I check my watch again. And at seven o'clock I ring the bell! Every morning except Sunday, I am the bell ringer. I have been ringing the bell since April 4, 1978, the day after I came to Copake, and I will continue to ring the bell, to be the bell ringer!

There is a lot of ice! Oh, no! There is a lot of ice in this bucket. How do I get the ice out, this ice out, so that I can pour the sap for the sugaring house? I need help! Oh, my goodness, this is too hard for me, this ice. Sugaring is important work, hard work; maybe this is too hard for me. Help! Gordon! Help! Oh, wait, I am doing it. I am loosening the ice. I did it!

I work at home. I cut the vegetables for the soup—the beans, the turnips, the onions, the leeks, the garlic, the carrots. I set the table. I fold our napkins. I am careful with the stove. I stir the soup. If there was no work, what would a person do? It would be boring! Before I came to Copake, at the other place, people sat around and did nothing. They watched television. It was boring!

These are three voices from Camphill Village, a therapeutic residential community near the town of Copake in upstate New York. In this community of 240 people, half are "villagers," people with developmental disabilities of one sort or another, who are valued, respected, and loved as whole humans by the other half of the community, who are called "co-workers." Together, villagers and co-workers create a community that integrates work life and home life, rest and prayer, music and dance.

reflections

I go to Camphill Village as often as I can, to visit my niece Katherine, who is a villager. Katherine was born with cerebral palsy and mental retardation. She was also born with a sense of humor and perspective, with determination and perseverance, with a capacity to reach out and to love. I go for the pace of life, for the pleasure of the community, and for the experience of integrity. I go because I discern the presence of God in the smell of the garlic being planted, in the support of one to another, in the colors of the candles being dipped, in holding one villager's hand, in a kiss on the cheek from another, in the good work that is accomplished day in and day out.

Work is at the heart of village life. Work serves the needs of the community, and the community serves the needs of each member. All work is meaningful, which is to say needed and valued by the community: to have the houses cleaned, the vegetables chopped, the tables set, the sap collected, the sugaring accomplished, the morning bell rung!

"Human work gives human dignity," one co-worker said recently. "Any contribution, no matter how large or small, is an expression of our common humanity, linking us to others for the sake of the whole." The daily schedule includes work in the morning and in the afternoon, six days a week.

The unique contribution of each individual is recognized, needed, valued, and encouraged to unfold, whether that of the young man whose personal challenges have brought him only recently to Camphill Village, or of Katherine, who was born with cerebral palsy and has lived in this village or other Camphill communities most of her life.

Katherine works in the bakery, kneading bread with her strong left hand and arm. At lunch, we sit down together for a meal of

reflections

delicious soup with herbs and vegetables, bread from Katherine's bakery, cheese from the dairy. Someone has sweetly and lovingly arranged a jelly glass of daisies and cosmos and ferns and placed it at the center of the table. We hold hands and say together, "May the meal be blessed."

After lunch there is time to rest before villagers and co-workers and the occasional visitor move on to the afternoon's work. I always think when I visit the village that the world outside would be kinder, gentler, wiser, and more effective if time was made each work day for an afternoon nap.

In a true sense, the Camphill Village community embodies the Christian ideal, or the Christian "real deal," which Paul sets forth in Romans 12: "Let love be genuine . . . hold fast to what is good; love one another with mutual affection; outdo one another in showing honor." There is no lagging in zeal at the village. Strangers such as I are extended generous hospitality. I visit to sink myself into the ideal, to be strengthened by the vision, to discern the presence of the Spirit of Life and Love celebrated in each aspect of daily life, to discern the presence of the healing and holy God, in which each person is valued and cherished and relations are cultivated with care.

Each person's work contributes to the common good. Each person's work reflects the work of the Creator. Work, rest, play, dance, thanksgiving, and music are not divided but woven seamlessly into the fabric of community life. Wendell Berry might have been describing life at Camphill Village in his sabbath poem "X": "When we work well, a Sabbath mood / Rests on our day, and finds it good."[3]

reflections

LIVING THE IDEAL OF CAMPHILL VILLAGE

How do we discern the presence of God in our own work and play when our schedules are so often intense? Can we take threads from the Camphill Village tapestry and weave them into our lives? I'd like to suggest three threads for consideration and conversation.

1. We need to be accepted as we are.

At Camphill Village, members of the community are valued, treasured, and respected, with all their strengths and vulnerabilities, joys and sadness, frustrations and anxieties, accomplishments and failure. This acceptance is in bold outline because villagers have developmental disabilities, many in multiple forms. But all humans, each of us, are also in need of acceptance. We experience joy and sadness, frustrations and fears. To accept the fullness and wholeness of each human, acceptance in self and other is a starting point. "Dream-singers all,"[4] proclaims Langston Hughes. All of us are children of the one God, no matter who we are or what we do.

2. We need work that has meaning and is valued by others.

This principle is true whether we are "landsmen, pins men, tinker or a tailor, a doctor, a lawyer, a soldier, or a sailor," as the folksong goes. Whether we are homemakers or corporate executives, teachers or technicians, we need a sense that our work has meaning and is valued. My niece Katherine kneads bread with her one good strong hand and arm; and when bread is served at the table, she receives thanks for her good part in that good loaf.

reflections

We honor one another by cultivating and expressing appreciation for the work of others: the colleague who shares an idea, the person who distributes the mail, the workers who clean our buildings. This appreciation strengthens the fabric of the community and honors individual contribution.

3. We need work that engages us.

We need work that gets us up in the morning, like that of the village bell ringer; work that on occasion stretches us and is too hard for us, like that of the village sap collector; work that sustains us through the day, like that of the village homemaker. Donald Hall, a poet laureate of the United States, has written an essay he calls "Lifework." In it, he writes that contentment is work so engrossing that you do not know you are working. He describes contentment in work as *absorbedness,* concentration on the work, total loss of identity, so that hours pass like seconds or without any notion of time elapsing.[5] I would add that the presence of the Creating God can be discerned when we are absorbed, engaged, and content in our life work.

PRAYER

Slow us down, O God of time and space, so that we may discern your presence in our life's work: in quiet moments, in our work with colleagues, in our creativity and productivity. Uphold us in our work so that we may offer it to you with thanksgiving. Amen.

reflections

FAITHFUL FRIENDS: WATCHING OVER ONE ANOTHER IN LOVE

Use this space to record thoughts, reflections, insights, prayer concerns, or other matters that arise from your weekly conversations with faithful friends.

—4—

Discerning God's Presence in the Shadows

PSALM FOR PRAYING

Psalm 42:1-3

As a deer longs for flowing streams,
   so my soul longs for you, O God.
My soul thirsts for God,
   for the living God.
When shall I come and behold
   the face of God?
My tears have been my food day and night,
while people say to me continually,
   "Where is your God?"

DAILY READINGS

DAY ONE
Matthew 5:1-12 *(The Beatitudes)*

DAY TWO
Luke 22:39-44 *(In his anguish he prayed more earnestly)*

DAY THREE
Jeremiah 29:11-14 *(When you search for me, you will find me)*

DAY FOUR

Romans 5:1-5 *(Hope does not disappoint us)*

DAY FIVE

Colossians 1:9-10 *(That you may be filled with understanding)*

DAY SIX

Read the chapter on pages 40–45. You may take notes in the space provided at the bottom of each page.

STRADDLING THE STREAMS, FINDING THE SOURCE

In the Appalachian mountains of Western Pennsylvania, tucked into the laurel ridge, is a little cabin with a good hearth and a wide porch where my family has spent weekends for three generations. On winter nights we watch the snow fall, silent and lovely, and anticipate the next day's cross country ski. When the day comes, we swish along mountain paths, down and up and around, past hemlocks that are snow laden. We see black-capped chickadees and nuthatches and redbirds, and an occasional deer.

In the spring, we search for trout lilies by the stream and the trailing arbutus near the wintergreen and the lichen. We plant lettuce and peas. We sit on the porch waiting for the bluebirds to return. They do. In the summer, we wake to the song of thrushes and rise to watch the mist moving through the valley.

We take picnics—chicken and deviled eggs and hand-squeezed lemonade—up to the mountain meadow. We read. We nap. In the evening, we watch the fireflies create magic in the fields and at the edge of the woods. In the fall, the witch hazel blossoms. The apples—McCoun, McIntosh, Delicious—are abundant in the orchard, and we pick them for sauce and for pies. We split wood for the coming winter, split and stack, split and stack, split and stack.

There is running water in the cabin, but it is too rusty for drinking or cooking. So no matter the season, winter or spring, summer or fall, each Friday evening when we arrive for the weekend, someone has to go to the mountain spring to get water. The spring is across the road and deep into the woods.

reflections

_____

_____

_____

_____

_____

As a child I was always reticent, even fearful, when it was my turn for this task: to take the ancient tin pitchers across the road and into the dark wood in the deep night; to straddle the stream, which is treacherously slippery; to wait while my eyes adjust to the pitch-dark night; to trust that the shadows are leaves rustling in the wind and not a fox or a bear or a brother out to scare me, which sometimes happens; to follow my feet to the source of our spring; to lean into the sound of the water while filling up the pitchers; and then finally, finally to turn toward the cabin, now lit up, and head home.

To discern the presence of God in the shadows is part of what it means to be a Christian—to be ready when life takes us into the dark places of human experience to the Source, to the Spring, to straddle the streams and adjust the eyes, to learn to trust, to learn to follow in faith that there will come a time to turn again toward the light.

The theological term for this process is *theodicy*: the relation of the good and loving God to the reality of the shadows and the dark; the presence of the strong and compassionate God amidst our anxieties and our disappointments, our sadness and our despair; the relation of the creative presence of God to human suffering and evil. Some theologians believe this task is paradoxical. I am inclined to refer to it as mystery—the mystery of the presence of God in the midst of the shadows and the dark.

The biblical witness is clear in relation to the mystery—that there are times in human experience when we cannot discern the presence of God, when God is absent, when God's face is hidden, when God forsakes us. The writer of Psalm 42 agonizes: "As a deer longs for flowing streams, / so my soul longs for you, O God. / My soul thirsts for God, / for the living God. / When shall I come

reflections

41

and behold / the face of God? My tears have been my food / day and night, / while people say to me continually, / 'Where is your God?' "

The absence referred to by the psalmist is not a momentary absence like a cloud passing over the sun. No, this absence is day after day and night after night. When the earliest disciples of Jesus tried to understand the reality of his death, what it meant to him and to them, they turned to the Hebrew Bible: "My God, my God, why have you forsaken me? / Why are you so far from helping me, from the words of my groaning?" (Psalm 22:1)

In the historical witness too we read of God's absence. Augustine writes of his restless heart, Saint John of the Cross of his own dark night of the soul. Hildegard composes a song yearning for celestial revelations. Dame Julian describes her fear of death before the Revelations. Simone Weil called her journal "Waiting for God."

On Christmas Eve 1966, Martin Luther King, Jr., tried to pray through his deep despair.[6] The experience of the absence of God, not being able to discern God in the shadows and the dark, is part of what it means to be a faithful witness.

Yet, and yet, on occasion while living in the shadows and the dark, we may be able to adjust our eyes, to be ready. We may be able to trust, to position, to listen. We may be able to straddle the stream and follow the water to its source.

EMBODYING THE PRESENCE OF GOD

As humans, we are able to position ourselves in the reality of God's absence, that we may be ready to discern God's presence once again. The psalmist positions himself by giving his soul a good talking-to. "Why are you cast down, O my soul, / and why are

reflections

42

you disquieted within me? / Hope in God" (Psalm 43:5). The psalmist positions himself in hope—the belief that the presence of God may be discernible or possible even in the shadows. Hope, as Dame Julian explains it, is the belief that all will be well, and every kind of thing will be well.

In the meantime, in the midst of the shadows and the dark, disciples are called to be the presence of God to one another, to be Love Incarnate, to witness with anything available to those who are in need of love. For instance, one August morning a number of years ago, my mother was sitting on the porch of our cabin, rocking back and forth in one of the rocking chairs, when two young friends, six-year-old Jenn and eight-year-old Tim, came skipping down the road. "Hello, Patty," they called.

Then they saw that my mother was weeping. "What's wrong, Patty?" asked Jenn. "You are crying, and your face is all red. Did you hurt yourself?"

"I don't know, Jenn," answered my mother. "I am just all full of sadness today."

The children held a whispered conference, then darted off together shouting, "Don't go anywhere. Stay put. We'll be right back!"

They did come back, though not right away. They were carrying a bucket in which were at least four or five frogs.

"We caught them down at the edge of the pond for you, Patty!" Tim proclaimed proudly.

Jenn added, "See how they go blink blink blink and croak croak croak. They will make you smile and maybe even be happy again."

In another instance, two students, Ashley and Kali, registered for a new course called Sub-Sahara Africa. "It sounded like something

reflections

different, interesting, cool," Ashley said in her deep Alabama drawl.

"We thought it might be an adventure," Kali added, "but we didn't expect that our lives would be changed for good."

But their lives did change as they began to study Darfur and the political, economic, sociological, and religious complexities of the situation there. Motivated by what they learned, they decided to mobilize the school community. Here is what they did in six short months:

- They made an impassioned presentation in an all-school meeting, with historical information and slides so that students could see the faces of the mothers and the children.
- After the meeting they had petitions ready for students to sign and send to their congressional representations.
- They sold T-shirts to raise money for the work of the American Red Cross in Darfur, researching first which organization had the most effective witness.
- They contacted a doctor who had been to Darfur with the organization Doctors Without Borders to give a lecture and answer questions.
- They carried out an inspirational and effective leaflet campaign to raise awareness and commitment, including one leaflet that said, "When your grandchildren ask you what you did to stop the genocide in Darfur, what will you tell them?"

Within the complex reality of evil and suffering in Darfur, in the shadows and the dark where the presence of God can hardly be discerned, Ashley and Kali, both seventeen years old, became the presence of God, seeking justice and being Love Incarnate—embodying the visible, tangible, creative, passionate love of God.

reflections

PRAYER

Energize us, O gracious God, so that we might discern your presence even in the shadows and the sadness. Enfold us in your love so that we might be your presence to others in the shadowy black darkness; for Jesus' sake, who bears our sadness and lightens the dark. Amen.

reflections

FAITHFUL FRIENDS: WATCHING OVER ONE ANOTHER IN LOVE

Use this space to record thoughts, reflections, insights, prayer concerns, or other matters that arise from your weekly conversations with faithful friends.

—5—

Discerning God's Presence in Our Habit of Being

PSALM FOR PRAYING

Psalm 119:33-37

Teach me, O Lord, the way of your statutes,
  and I will observe it to the end.
Give me understanding, that I may keep your law
  and observe it with my whole heart.
Lead me in the path of your commandments,
  for I delight in it.
Turn my heart to your decrees,
  and not to selfish gain.
Turn my heart from looking at vanities;
  give me life in your ways.

DAILY READINGS

DAY ONE
Genesis 1:26-31 *(God made humans in God's own image)*

DAY TWO
Matthew 25:34-40 *(Unto the least of these)*

DAY THREE
Psalm 19:7-14 *(The law of the Lord)*

DAY FOUR

Luke 10:25-37 *(Who is my neighbor?)*

DAY FIVE

Ephesians 3:16-21 *(Rooted and grounded in love)*

DAY SIX

Read the chapter on pages 50–55 You may take notes in the space provided at the bottom of each page.

LEARNING TO TEACH

I spent much of the summer before I began teaching at the Lawrenceville School talking to people who had taught, asking for hints, their best instincts, any helpful advice. One person said, "A good teacher knows her subject thoroughly," which seemed sensible except for the fact that I was teaching world religions, and my knowledge of Hinduism and Buddhism was superficial at best. (Does anyone know how to pronounce *Sanatana Dharma?* know what distinguishes Therevada Buddhism from Mahayana Buddhism?)

Another teacher said, "Remember, Sue Anne, you only need to be one day ahead of them," which turned out to be true more often than I would care to admit. Another experienced teacher, a true mentor in the art and craft of teaching, reflected, "They can smell fear!"

I was indeed frightened—awed, really—by where I had landed myself, or rather where God had landed me. At fifty-four years old, teaching for the first time, I had a smile on my face but was shaking in my shoes.

On the first day of teaching I stood in my classroom at the Harkness Table, a large dining-room-like table for fourteen students that is the hallmark of the Lawrenceville teaching method. The students began to come in and take their places at the table. I greeted each one.

A bold young man named Andrew came in with a twinkle in his eye and a mischievous grin. He tossed his Red Sox cap on the table and announced, "There's one thing I want to know! Do you need to be religious to take a world religions course? Because you might as well know from the start, I am not religious."

reflections

50

I panicked, of course, wondering how to respond. Then I remembered, from my one-day faculty orientation session, that the idea was to return questions to the whole class, the magic of Harkness Table teaching.

"I don't know," I said. "Class, what do you think? Is it better to practice a faith when we are studying world religions? Or is it better to be nonreligious like Andrew here, which may give some objectivity to the learning process?"

The students loved this question and debated it for nearly the entire class period. My fears subsided slightly, and I thought to myself, "I am going to like it here."

I teach two sections of world religions each term. The course introduces students to the basic themes and teachings of five of the world's religions: Hinduism, Buddhism, Judaism, Christianity, and Islam. We have a textbook called *Living Religions*. We have a collection of primary sources. We have a conversation with one who practices each of the religions. We attend various prayer services, worship, and meditation. We watch DVDs. I hope that the students gain the understanding each religion has of God, along with the scriptures, the purpose and direction the religion gives its followers, the role of social justice in each faith, the holy days and sacred practices, and what it means to be part of each religious faith community.

We also learn the moral code of each religion. Four years into teaching, I may, in fact, have developed a modest reputation in this regard—we learn the codes together in class as a community of learners. The learning methods may be a little upbeat, somewhat silly, or inspirational to make them more interesting than rote memorization.

For Hinduism we explore the Code of Manu and discuss the meaning of *satyam* (integrity), *brahamcharya* (self-control), and

reflections

51

ahimsa (nonviolence). For Buddhism we explore the Four Noble truths and the Eightfold Path. For Judaism we learn the Shema Israel and the Ten Commandments. For Christianity it is the Beatitudes and the parable of the good Samaritan. For Islam we learn the Five Pillars.

Then, in their final and most important journal entry, students of world religions write their own moral code. Examples have included the fourteen principles of Peter, a musical moral code by Marina, Jillian's guidelines for life, and the elevenfold path of goodness without religion by (who else?) Andrew.

A HABIT OF BEING

What does it mean to live within the moral code of a faith community, to come to understand the dimension of holy intention for each of our lives and our life together, and to discern the will of God, which is good and acceptable and perfect, as Paul puts it in his Letter to the Romans?

In Marcus Borg's *Reading the Bible Again for the First Time: Taking the Bible Seriously But Not Literally* (and, I would add, taking the Bible joyfully), Borg probes the dimensions of the two Creation narratives at the beginning of Genesis. He then puts forth what he considers their central truth claim: "The universe and we [are] ... grounded in the sacred. 'This' is utterly remarkable and wondrous, a Mystery beyond words that evokes wonder, awe, and praise. We begin our lives 'in paradise,' but we all experience expulsion into a world of exile, anxiety, self-preoccupation, bondage, and conflict. And yes, also a world of goodness and beauty: it is the creation of God. But it is a world in which something is awry."[7]

reflections

Borg reminds us that we are made in the image of God and the biblical story is our story. Living east of Eden now, we long to find wholeness and holiness, to center ourselves in God who creates, redeems, and sustains us. But how are we to fulfill this longing?

Thomas Aquinas in his *Summa Theologica* (eighteen volumes on Christian theology and practice) coins the phrase "habit of being" to describe how the Christian life develops. How do we develop a habit of being so that we might discern the presence of God in our individual lives and in our life together, as disciples of Jesus and stewards of God's mystery? I imagine there are as many possible responses as there are Christians, past and present. I will close with a few who have inspired me in my habit of being.

Mississippi John Hurt

Legend has it that an enthusiastic pupil of Andres Segovia once played a solo recording of blues guitarist Mississippi John Hurt's piece "I Shall Not Be Moved" for the great classical teacher. Entranced, Segovia wondered aloud, "And who was the second guitar?"

John Hurt was born in Avalon, Mississippi, at the edge of the Mississippi Delta, one of ten children. When he was nine years old, his mother bought him a Black Ann guitar for $1.50. In a short time, he had taught himself to play. When someone asked him how he made his melodies, he responded, "Well, sir, I just get up from my prayers and make it sound like I think it ought to."

When Hurt worked as a field hand and labored at picking cotton and corn, he would take a break and pick up his guitar. When he worked with cattle or on the railroad or the river, he would do the same. He played the guitar on the front stoop of the Carroll County Valley Store and sometimes at local dances or church suppers.

reflections

Misssissippi John Hurt's habit of being was working hard and making music, sweet songs for the Lord.

Kelsey Sullivan

Kelsey Sullivan, a rising junior at Lawrenceville, has bright blue eyes, a sweet smile, a darling giggle, and a passion for community service.

"I found out early on what I was going to do!" she says. While other students went to Vail to ski for spring vacation, or to the Caribbean to sail, Kelsey went to Biloxi, Mississippi, to scrape mold out of homes that had been water soaked by Hurricane Katrina. As soon as school was out for the summer, she returned to Biloxi for another two weeks.

Kelsey went to Costa Rica to volunteer in a village, teaching children and helping to develop a strategy for eco-tourism. She went to the Lawrenceville School camp to lead a cabin of seven girls who were bright with energy and promise but came from underserved communities.

Kelsey says, "It's amazing to be with these girls—not always easy but always amazing. Tya was afraid of ants and bugs of any kind. Perhaps if we worked through that fear it would help her deal with her other fears. Shiara would not go near the water. Then one day I took Shiara's hand, and we entered the water together. Before we finished, Shiara had learned to float."

Kelsey Sullivan's habit of being is service to others.

Dan-el Padilla Peralta

Dan-el Padilla Peralta was born in the Dominican Republic and came to the United States when he was four years old. His parents had a temporary nonimmigrant visa granted so that his mother

reflections

could get a medical treatment she needed in New York City. Dan-el's childhood was defined on one hand by the difficulties his parents faced—finding employment, making ends meet, coping with his mother's illness, finding places to live—and on the other hand by his mother's strong faith. At a point in his early adolescence, a social worker at a Salvation Army shelter guided him toward the Collegiate School, a private institution in Manhattan. There, Dan-el says, he was introduced to the classics, which "offered a window into another world, a kind of respite from the more crushing aspects of the life I was living." Academics soothed him. "I think often of Helen Vendler's remarks in a *Paris Review* about the importance of poetry. . . . Lyric and verse can be faithful lifelong companions, personal resources, aids in times of anxiety and distress."[8]

Dan-el Padilla Peratta was Princeton University's Class of 2006 salutatorian. He developed a habit of being in classics.

How do you begin to discern the presence of God in your own life, through your own habit of being? Perhaps the examples of Mississippi John Hurt, Kelsey Sullivan, and Dan-el Padilla Peratta will help you discover it.

PRAYER

Lead us, Spirit of God, into your presence,
Into the blessing of your wisdom,
Good humor, and perspective
So that our habit of being
Might be fully in your joy.
Amen.

_____
_____
_____
_____
_____

reflections

FAITHFUL FRIENDS: WATCHING OVER ONE ANOTHER IN LOVE

Use this space to record thoughts, reflections, insights, prayer concerns, or other matters that arise from your weekly conversations with faithful friends.

—6—

Planning the Next Steps Together

Psalm 19:7, 9b-10

The law of the LORD is perfect,
    reviving the soul;
the decrees of the LORD are sure,
    making wise the simple;
            . . .
the ordinances of the LORD are true
    and righteous altogether.
More to be desired are they than gold,
    even much fine gold;
sweeter also than honey,
    and drippings of the honeycomb.

FOR THE PAST FEW WEEKS you have experienced the "Come and See" portion of this study, exploring aspects of the Christian character trait of discernment. You have learned about and reflected upon "Discerning God's Presence in Our Midst," "Discerning God's Presence in Our Work," "Discerning God's Presence in the Shadows," and "Discerning God's Presence in Our Habit of Being." You have experienced psalms for praying and lectio divina to engage Scripture in a prayerful way. You have communicated regularly as faithful friends with another person in the group. You have learned all this in the company of other Christians who also seek God's "good life."

In the following space, take some time now to write about particular learnings from the previous sessions that have been meaningful or significant to you.

The time has come to move from understanding discernment to developing practices of discernment. It is time to "Go and Do" discernment in your group.

At your next session, you and your group will plan together how to "try out" what you have learned about the Christian character trait of discernment. Then, for the weeks to follow, you will put your plan into action, both as individuals and as a group.

Your group planning session will be most effective if each member, in preparation for the session, takes a few minutes to brainstorm ways in which the group can begin to practice discernment over the next six weeks during the "Go and Do" portion of the study.

On the pages that follow, you will see several boxes, each of which contains an idea prompt. These idea prompts are designed to help you imagine ways in which you and your group could put into practice what you have learned about discernment. Allow your mind to explore every possible avenue for embodying this notion of discernment in your life as a Christian. Resist the tendency to edit your ideas; instead, record all of them in the spaces provided. Be ready to share them with the group when you meet.

As you consider and record your ideas, keep in mind that ideas are only a part of Christian character. Christianity comes alive only when, inspired by ideas, we move into the world, practicing and embodying our faith. That's when we truly become the body of Christ and begin—haltingly at first but then with confidence and faith—living the good life together.

Lectio divina Scripture passages

Behavioral changes to make

Ministry events to consider

Mission work to conceive and implement

Speakers to invite

Field trips, retreats, pilgrimages to take

Books to read, movies to see

Other ideas

Endnotes

1. From *The Varieties of Religious Experience: A Study in Human Nature*, by William James (Modern Library Paperback Edition, 2002); page 61.
2. From "Psalm Eight" in *The Death of Adam*, by Marilynne Robinson (Picador, 2005); page 243.
3. From *Sabbaths*, by Wendell Berry (North Point Press, 1987); page 19.
4. From "Laughers," by Langston Hughes in *The Collected Poems of Langston Hughes*, edited by Arnold Rampersad and David Roessel (Knopf, 1994); pages 27–28.
5. From *Life Work*, by Donald Hall (Beacon Press, 2003); page 23.
6. From notes taken at a Martin Luther King, Jr., address at The Lawrenceville School (New Jersey) on January 15, 2004.
7. From *Reading the Bible Again for the First Time: Taking the Bible Seriously but Not Literally*, by Marcus Borg (HarperSanFrancisco, 2001); pages 80–81.
8. From "My American Dream" (*The Princeton Alumni Weekly*, vol. 6/ no. 14, June 7, 2006); page 16.

ACKNOWLEDGMENTS

Living the Good Life Together: A Study of Christian Character in Community is the result of a very good idea. The idea was that the church needed help in teaching God's people to cultivate patterns or practices of holy living—in other words, to learn to live a good life as defined by Scripture and exemplified by Jesus. This idea became the subject of a very fruitful conversation, thanks especially to the participation of Timothy W. Whitaker, Resident Bishop of the Florida Annual Conference of The United Methodist Church; L. Gregory Jones, Dean and Professor of Theology at Duke University Divinity School; and Paul W. Chilcote, Professor of Historical Theology and Wesleyan Studies at Asbury Theological Seminary in Florida. Their commitment to the idea and their contributions to the development process provided the vision and the impetus for this unique resource.